The Key to Peace

by Sri Swami Satchidananda

Library of Congress Cataloging in
Publication Data
Satchidananda, Swami.
Key to Peace

I. Title.
2011
ISBN 978-0-932040-12-1

Copyright © 2011
by Satchidananda Ashram–Yogaville, Inc.
All rights reserved, including the right to reproduce
this book or portions thereof in any form.

Printed in the United States of America.

Integral Yoga® Publications
Satchidananda Ashram–Yogaville
108 Yogaville Way, Buckingham, VA, USA 23921
www.YogaAndPeace.org

Yogaville, Virginia, USA

Books by Sri Swami Satchidananda

Beyond Words	Heaven on Earth
Enlightening Tales	Integral Yoga Hatha
The Golden Present	Kailash Journal
Bound To Be Free: The Liberating Power of Prison Yoga	The Living Gita
	To Know Your Self
The Healthy Vegetarian	Yoga Sutras of Patanjali

Titles in this special Peter Max cover art series:

Meditation	How to Find Happiness
The Key to Peace	The Be-Attitudes
Overcoming Obstacles	Everything Will Come to You
Adversity and Awakening	Thou Art That: How to Know Yourself
Satchidananda Sutras	
Gems of Wisdom	Free Yourself
Pathways to Peace	The Guru Within

*Books/Films about
Sri Swami Satchidananda*

Sri Swami Satchidananda:
   Biography of a Yoga Master

Sri Swami Satchidananda:
   Portrait of a Modern Sage

The Master's Touch

Boundless Giving: The Life and Service of
Sri Swami Satchidananda

Living Yoga: The life and teachings of
   Swami Satchidananda (DVD)

Many Paths, One Truth: The Interfaith
   Message of Swami Satchidananda (DVD)

The Essence of Yoga:
   The Path of Integral Yoga with
   Swami Satchidananda (DVD)

For complete listing of books, CDs and DVDs:
www.iydbooks.com

Dedication

Dedication. What a perfect word this is to begin *The Key to Peace*. Sri Swami Satchidanandaji led a life of total, inspiring dedication; and dedication is what this booklet is about.

More than sixty years ago, Sri Swami Satchidananda was initiated into the Holy Order of *Sannyas* by his spiritual master Sri Swami Sivanandaji Maharaj. With these monastic vows, Sri Gurudev (as he is called by his students) began a formal commitment to a life of total dedication to all creation.

Sometimes people wonder if a life of renunciation means a life of somber inactivity. One had only to observe Sri Gurudev to have seen that quite the reverse was true. Always the essence of real joy, fun and freedom, he awakened the same qualities in those whose lives were touched by him and his teachings. A dynamic servant of all humanity, he continues to be the personification of compassion, wisdom, ease and peace.

How did he attain this wonderful state? How can we attain the same peace? In this booklet Sri Gurudev gives us the key.

Integral Yoga Publications® is happy to offer the revised version of *The Key to Peace* (originally published in 1976) in honor of Guru Poornima and in celebration of Sri Swami Satchidananda's numerous years of formally declared selfless and joyous service. We will forever be grateful recipients of that service.

Integral Yoga Publications
Satchidananda Ashram–Yogaville
Buckingham, Virginia
February, 2011

Contents

The Forbidden Fruit 1

Selflessness 7

Use, But Don't Possess 9

Be Always Happy 17

The Greatest Mantra 23

What is the Goal of Yoga? 25

Just Keep Giving 27

Equip Yourself to Serve 29

Real Service 33

Everything is Equally Dignified 39

Joy is Your Reward 47

God's Business 53

Love to Serve 57

About the Author 63

The Forbidden Fruit

I say the selfless person is the most selfish person. Why? You are selfless because you don't want to disturb your peace. You know that by being selfless, you will always retain your happiness. A selfish person can never be happy. Know that. This is the fundamental teaching of all the religions and of Yoga.

If you want to summarize the essence of all religious teachings and put it in one word, that word is: selflessness. Be dedicated. Sacrifice is the law of life. What does the Cross teach us? Sacrifice.

What does a flower teach us? Sacrifice. The tree sacrifices its flower to produce a fruit; the candle burns itself away to give us light. There is sacrifice everywhere. The entire nature demonstrates the benefit of sacrifice.

Look at the apple tree. It gives us thousands of fruits. If you ask the tree,

"How many fruits did you give this season?"

"Oh, several thousands."

"Ah, did people come and beg you for them?"

"No, I don't wait for that. I just give."

"Without their even asking?"

"Yes. That's my nature. I find it a joy to give that way."

"Suppose nobody comes to take them?"

"That's their business. I don't want to eat my own fruit so I just drop it."

"But your apples are so delicious.

Don't you at least try one?"

If you have the ears to hear, you will hear the tree laughing at you.

"Don't think I'm a human being to taste my own fruit. Only human beings run after the fruits, and that is why they are in misery."

The tree will tell you this. It not only gives its fruit to those who praise it, but even to those who stone it.

Throw a stone at an apple tree and you'll get even more fruits. Throw a stone at a person and you know what you'll get! So who is greater, the apple tree or the human tree? When I walk around and see an apple tree, I feel humbled.

So don't expect anything. If you make an appointment for some result, you must be ready to face disappointment. Ask for nothing; just serve. That way you will retain your peace, because peace is always in you; it's not something that comes from outside. As long as you don't disturb it by your expectations and anxieties, it will be there.

The best way not to disturb it is to not expect anything in return for your actions and to just give what you can. You needn't even bother to know whether a person appreciates or benefits by your service or not. Giving is your business, that's all.

That is renunciation or dedication. When you renounce the attachment and expectation of the fruits of your actions, you retain your peace. That fruit is the forbidden fruit, let us remember that. God commanded Adam not to eat the fruit, but it is not just that once upon a time in the Garden of Eden an apple was forbidden to that one person. No, we are all Adams and we are all planting trees. Every action is a tree and every action bears its fruit. We are asked not to eat that fruit; but, instead, offer it to humanity.

The *Bhagavad Gita* says: *Ashaantasya kutah sukham,* which means, "How can someone be happy if he or she has not found peace?" Then it gives the answer also: *Tyaagat shaantir anantaram,* "The dedicated ever enjoy supreme peace." How can there be happiness without peace? And what is the way to that peace? Dedication, sacrifice.

Our entire life, our very living itself must be for the sake of others. Eat for the sake of others, breathe for the sake of others. Then nobody in the world can disturb your peace. It is guaranteed.

In some way or other we must renounce. It doesn't mean you must become a monk or nun to be a renunciate or selfless servant. Sacrifice is what we are learning even in a family life.

Once you have a partner, you have to sacrifice at least fifty percent to that partner, is it not so? Otherwise you can't make a good home. Then, you both must sacrifice for the sake of the little ones. So our own lives can teach us how to sacrifice. That is the key for every religion and for Yoga as well.

Selflessness

Selflessness is the message of every religion. Be selfless, be dedicated. Keeping the mind clean is true Yoga–that is the purpose of the Yoga practices, of meditation.

Selflessness is the key to spiritual life. All the religious people, every seeker, every prophet, every sage has sacrificed his or her selfishness for the sake of humanity.

That is why you respect, worship and adore them. You want to follow them. A selfish person is never followed or respected like that.

Maybe as long as a person is in power you salute him or her–out of fear probably, not gratitude. But a selfless person is loved and respected by the whole world, wherever he or she goes.

I often suggest this practice: try for just one week to be completely selfless. Do every action as a service. Have a sample "selfless week." "For the whole week let me be selfless. Let me always give, give, give and love, love, love."

If you really don't get any benefit, if you don't enjoy that week, okay, go back to your old way. But if you get even a taste of that joy of giving for the sake of giving, you will love that and you will want to taste that joy more and more. You will look for opportunities to taste that again and again. I guarantee it.

Use, But Don't Possess

What is Yoga? People often think it means standing on the head, doing some physical postures and breathing or some meditation.

But, in simple words, Yoga means keeping the mind calm and clean to reflect the peace and joy which is in you as your True Self.

Whatever helps you do that can be called Yoga. In other words, any action that will not disturb your mind is a yogic action.

On the physical level, we talk about wrong food, wrong drink, wrong air and wrong habits disturbing the ease of the body.

In the same way, wrong thinking will disturb the mind. What kind of thinking is that? When you feel your mind is disturbed, why is it? Anxiety, fear, worry, disappointment, hatred, jealousy and so on. There can be a big list. But I say there is just one cause behind all those disturbances–your selfishness.

Take fear, for example. Of what are you afraid? Of losing something to which you are attached. If you have a lot of money in the safe, even at midnight you will get up to see whether the safe is still locked or not.

You are afraid of losing the money. Instead, if you feel, "It is with me now. As long as it is here, I may use it. If by chance it is taken away, I won't be disturbed." Then you won't have any fear of losing it because you are not attached to it.

So the cause of your fear is your selfish attachment: "I want it for me." If you are selfless, if you are not attached to anything, you need not be afraid of anything. The same applies to all our mental disturbances.

If you are not selfish, you will not be anxious about anything, you will never worry about anything; there will be no need to hate anyone or be jealous or angry or disappointed.

That is why all the religious scriptures say, "Don't possess anything. Lead a detached life."

Say, "I am Thine, All is Thine," instead of "Everything should be mine." That's why I make a pun on the word "mine."

If you put a lot of "mines" around you, they will wait to explode. Your peace is constantly in danger of being disturbed. So change all the "mines" to "Thine" and you will be safe.

But you may ask, "If I am not to be attached to things and people, why should I do anything? What benefit is there in having or doing anything?" Here we should know that things are with us for our use, not for us to possess.

When I give a talk, I come in, they give me a nice seat to sit on and a microphone. I can certainly say they are mine during that time. But when I finish the talk, can I take the chair and microphone and go? No.

They are only mine as long as I am using them. If you are a secretary in an office, you will be given a desk, computer, pens and files. You will say, "This is my computer." But if you are fired, can you take the computer and go? No.

In the same way, we are all hired here in this life to do certain jobs. In this big "office," God or the Cosmic Force is the manager. God gives us typewriters, cars, houses, husbands, wives, children, friends and experiences according to our merits. But when the time comes for us to be "fired," when the Divine Proprietor feels we have finished our jobs, we have to leave everything and go.

Has anybody ever taken his or her car to the cremation grounds? You can't take anything with you. You came alone and you go alone. In between many things are given to you. If you just use them and then let them go, your mind will never be disturbed.

Anybody who renounces selfish attachment and lives a neutral life, seeing everybody equally, serving everybody equally, without any personal attachment, is called a saintly person or holy person because his or her mind is always calm and clean. Someone like that is always happy. So lead a detached, dedicated life. Do your duty well, but never expect specific results from your actions.

If I go to speak somewhere with the desire and expectation of establishing a Yoga center in that place, then I would not be there just to serve everyone but to catch some "fish."

Even while I was talking, I would be anxious, I would watch the faces—who will be the right fish to be caught in my net? Then I would be trying to do two things at once.

My service would not be complete or perfect then. My mind would be split. I would be anxious, "Who is smiling at me? Who is appreciating me?" That anxiety would disturb my mind.

And suppose after the talk nobody got into my net, I would be disappointed. See, all these emotions would be there if I came with a personal motive.

If not, I am just there, I share what little I know. If it suits you, take it. If not, drop it and go. I neither gain nor lose anything either way, but I retain my peace and joy.

I am there, neither for gain nor loss but just to serve. If we perform all our actions like this, as a service, without expecting the results or fruits of the actions, the mind will be calm and clean, peaceful and joyful.

Be Always Happy

I learned the value of selflessness very early in my life. I was like you—I had been a student and also worked in many business fields. Like other people, I also wanted everything to happen for me.

Whenever anybody got in my way, I got disappointed. And the more I gained, the more greedy I became. I wanted more and more. There were no limitations.

Then I said, "What is this life I'm leading? When am I going to be satisfied? The more I get, the more I want. There's no end. Okay, no more! Let me be contented with what I have."

And, even with that, "Let me use everything for the sake of others. Whatever I have—money or possessions or intelligence or physical energy—I will just use them for the benefit of all and be happy."

What is the nature of a contented mind? Always balanced. Always peaceful. Contentment is golden. Always say: "Enough."

That means you never want anything. Not that you get everything and say, "I am above wants."

The real way to raise above wants is not to want anything. If it comes, let it come. If it goes, wonderful, let it go. Attachments are what bind us. The more attachments we have, the greater the bondage; no attachment, no bondage.

Let things come and go. You are not after them. You don't run after things. If they run after you, all right.

The more you run after things, the more they go away. Instead, say, "Okay, I am not running after anything. I am here. I am contented."

Then, everything comes to you. Everything looks for a contented person. Because everything and everybody likes to be with a contented person.

When there is a nice fragrance, when there is honey in you, you don't have to advertise for the bees to come to you. They just come.

A contented mind is always balanced, above likes and dislikes. All our problems are caused either by likes or by dislikes.

When you like something, you dream of it, you look for it and you are anxious.

If you dislike something you go through turmoil. So discriminate with this question: "Will this help me to maintain my peace?"

Yes. And that is how I train people also: "Come on, serve your brothers and sisters. Don't just sell everything; don't make it a business. Just do what you can.

If they see something beautiful and feel you should be given something for your effort, let them give." Certainly the heart of every person has a soft corner somewhere.

People recognize good things. Even the worst person has a soft corner in his or her heart.

If you show people love, they will recognize it. Animals can feel your love; can't a human being?

I feel that by loving service you can conquer the whole world. You can be a good friend to all.

You can always be happy. And I have been enjoying that happiness, that peace for the past so many years. I am never disappointed.

The Greatest Mantra

Question: Do you use a mantra, Gurudev?

Sri Gurudev: My mantra is to see that I spend every breath in serving others. The constant remembrance of the dedication, of the sacrifice is the greatest mantra for me.

The human tendency is to think of "me" first, and then of others. But if we turn it the other way around, "you" first and "me" next, only then can we be happy always.

That is *tyaga* or dedication. For such a person, there is eternal peace; nothing can disturb him or her.

Because we all want peace. The ultimate goal is peace or happiness. It is in our hands. God helps those who help themselves.

What is the Goal of Yoga?

Serenity of mind. But you can't keep the mind serene just by sitting and meditating an hour then going out and doing anything you want with all selfish and greedy intentions.

I would say that you don't even need to meditate. My own experience is this: I don't do asanas, I don't meditate, I don't do anything that I ask you to do.

All I do is to just live for the sake of others. I do everything for the benefit of the humanity, for the benefit of the people. And so, I am young, I am happy, I am peaceful. That's my secret.

It's good to do asanas, to meditate and prepare yourself in your personal life. But what is the goal? Ultimately, to serve others. What do you need to serve others?

A clean body, a calm mind, a sharp intellect. You are preparing yourself. Even preparing yourself becomes a service to others. Take as much time as you want to prepare yourself. But the goal is ultimately to use yourself in others' service.

Keep this in mind: "I am here to serve; I am doing everything to serve others." Why are you eating? Not to develop the biceps and triceps; you are eating to gain enough energy to serve others. Why are you going to sleep? You are tired, you can't serve, you have to go and rest well, then get up fresh to serve others. The goal is, "I am preparing myself to serve others." So, your service to yourself becomes others' service. Whatever you do, that should be your ultimate goal, then it is a service always.

Just Keep Giving

You might ask how you could survive if you always think of serving others. But if you keep giving, you will be taken care of.

If a cow gives milk, won't the cowherd take care of her? If she doesn't give milk, what would he do? Simply dispose of her.

If a tree brings forth a lot of fruit, we take good care of it. We pour more water, nourish it, put a fence around it. But if it is not bearing fruit? "Unnecessary, chop it down."

So you don't need to worry about getting things for yourself. Just keep giving, and the world that receives everything from you will take good care of you because it won't want to lose your service.

If it doesn't feel that way then what are you doing here? You're a burden on the earth then. If we can't be useful to people, let's say goodbye and go. Let our place be occupied by somebody else. That should be our attitude.

From one lit candle another candle receives the light. The first candle is still the same. It doesn't get diminished by giving light to another candle. That is what is said in the *Upanishads*:

> "That is full; this also is full.
>
> This fullness came from that Fullness.
>
> Though this Fullness came from that Fullness,
>
> That Fullness remains forever full."

Equip Yourself to Serve

Question: It sounds very nice to serve without expecting anything in return, but what if one has to earn a living or support a family?

Answer: Earning a living and supporting a family need not be a selfish action. It can also be Karma Yoga (selfless service).

What do you do with your salary? It provides food, clothing, a house. And why do you want to eat, why dress, why a house? Why do you want to live at all? To serve others.

If you are living to serve, don't you need to eat? You have to fill up the gas tank so the car will run. You have to keep the engine greased and the car washed. You need a garage for the car. Your own body is the same. And can you do that without a salary? With that money you equip yourself with enough energy to give energy back to others. Even your eating, sleeping, and drinking become Karma Yoga if you do it with that intention: "I am keeping myself fit to serve others. If not, I don't need to sleep or eat; I don't even need to live."

If that feeling is there and if your salary is not going to take care of your true need (rather than the greed!) you can even demand a bigger salary.

Tell your boss, "I am serving you. But this money is not enough; I must have more." An employer should know the needs of the employees.

But if he or she doesn't know that, you can always demand. Yes, and you are still a Karma Yogi if you do it with the right attitude.

You can't say you are getting something in return for your work. Even the so-called return goes back to others. So the entire life becomes Karma Yoga: You live for the sake of others, serving God and the creation every minute with every breath.

Your very work becomes worship. Your every act is part of that worship of the Supreme manifest as this world. We should understand our daily activities in that light.

Real Service

All our resentment and other troubles come because we think too much of ourselves. If we don't think of ourselves, there is no room for these problems.

When we want to be spiritual seekers, the first thing we should do is forget ourselves. Never, never think of yourself: "Where will I sleep, what will I eat, what will I get for me?" "I, I, I" should be forgotten.

Instead, always occupy yourself in some service. "I have so many things to do, I don't even have time to think of myself."

That should be the attitude. Somebody else should come and worry: "You've been working for the past sixteen hours. You must eat something. Come on."

We see such service; it's not just a philosophy. I have seen many people doing things that way. Others had to go and force them to stop and eat. They would say, "Oh no, no, I have to finish these letters now."

Sometimes they used to sit and type until midnight in Sivananda Ashram in Rishikesh. Somebody had to send tea there, and even then the tea would get cold sitting beside them. They wouldn't even remember to drink it.

If you keep your eye on your work, you do not know sleep, or hunger or hear what others are talking about. When you get immersed in your service, you don't have time to worry about yourself.

That is real service. If you always put yourself first: "Me first. If I don't get this, I won't do this service," then it's not service. You get, you return; it's a business then.

Instead, you should be the last person. If there's nothing more to be done, then you can say, "Oh, there's nothing more to do. I haven't eaten anything. Probably I should eat something now." If on your way to the kitchen, you come across an opportunity to serve, forget the food and start serving.

If you call it a spiritual practice, this attitude will come without any doubt if you enjoy your service. If you don't enjoy it, everything will be heavy on your shoulders. "Oh, I have to do it. Can't they find someone else for this? Am I the only person who is available?"

It becomes a burden to you, and it's not selfless service then. There's nothing spiritual there. If you call it a spiritual practice or service or Karma Yoga, it should give you the maximum joy. If it doesn't, it's just a selfish act.

If your action is motivated by doing something for others, for bringing benefit to others and not expecting any result or reward for yourself, such an action is called Karma Yoga.

Here, we should think of another point also. You don't need to pick and choose what service you want to do. "I will enjoy only this and not that."

Service is service, wherever and whatever it is. Why this and not that? In what way are they different?

Why should you think one is superior and the other inferior? "I'll take care of my eyes, but not my legs." Okay, you take care of your eyes and wear nice glasses, but if you want to see something beautiful, you need the legs to take you there. If you don't take care of the legs, you can't even go there.

We were not created to have our own selfish lives. We were created to serve others. That is the purpose of Karma Yoga.

The rain doesn't pour down for itself. The sun doesn't shine for itself. Everything in the nature exists to serve others.

Everything is Equally Dignified

For a spiritual seeker, everything is beautiful. It doesn't matter what you do, where you are.

From the shrine to the toilet, from the garden to the kitchen, whether you use a pen or an axe, everything is equally important and equally dignified and all a worthy field for your service.

Whether people appreciate your actions or not, even if they criticize you for it, that is their business. You have done your job.

You are satisfied with what you have done; you did it to your capacity and you don't expect anything in return, so your mind is always calm. That is Yoga, calmness of mind.

Either do your service for others, with the thought, "It's our home, our city, our world," or do it as God's service, "All for Jesus or all for Allah or all for Krishna."

It may be difficult to always do something for others or for the whole community. Perhaps you don't respect and love everybody that much.

Maybe you would wash a few clothes for a person you love, but if you see some other person's clothing also mixed in and if you don't like that person, you might say, "Oh my goodness, must I wash all these things?"

You differentiate because you don't love everybody equally. So when you can't do it for humanity, do it in the name of God. "I am living in God's home. Every foot of ground on which I step belongs to God. Every tool I use belongs to God.

The kitchen is God's; the typewriter belongs to God; the altar is God's; the tools and the garden belong to God. All these people are God's children. Through everything I am serving God."

And why do you want to serve God? "Because that is the only way to put my little self out of the way so that I can get God's blessings and peace. Only through service can I brush aside my ego and petty limitations."

See how the whole philosophy comes in just in the path of service? That's why a person may not study anything, may not do anything, may not even sit and meditate, may not do Hatha Yoga, but just serve in whatever way he or she can.

Mere service, nothing else, is enough for your yogic or spiritual practice. That keeps your heart so clean, and that is everything. And it even takes care of your health.

When you serve that well, you get real hunger; you eat well, you digest well, you sleep well. There's a peace in the mind and an ease in the body.

"*Karma Yogam ondre nammai kakkum ennum Vedam,*" said a Tamil saint. "Karma Yoga alone is enough to save us all is the essence of the scriptures."

That means all the scriptures ultimately come down to one best practice–Karma Yoga, selfless service.

We are always working in one way or another. So to make your work a service becomes a constant practice. For meditation you have to come to an altar and only at certain times. You can't be sitting quietly in meditation always. For

Hatha Yoga postures (*asanas*) you have a certain time limit. For eating you have a time limit.

But for Karma Yoga there's no time limit. From morning to evening you are doing some action so everything can be Karma Yoga. Your walking, typing, talking and eating are themselves Karma Yoga.

So you become a constant practitioner. You don't limit your practice of this Yoga to a certain time.

You are a yogi at all times, not just in the morning or the evening or at noon or when you repeat your mantra.

You are a yogi throughout your day, throughout your life. Everything becomes Karma Yoga. This is what Lord Krishna taught to Arjuna in the *Bhagavad Gita*:

> *"Yatkaroshi yadasnaasi*
> *yajjuhoshi dadaasi yat;*
> *yat tapasyasikaunteya*
> *tat kurushva madarpanam."*
> –*Bhagavad Gita*, IX:27

"Whatever you do, whatever you eat, whatever you offer in sacrifice, whatever you give, whatever austerity you practice, do it as an offering to Me."

Because everything is doing, is it not? You do worship, you do meditation, you do *asanas*, you do walk, do talk, do your *pranayama*–do, do, do. When you say "do," it means action.

So every action should be selfless, then you're a Karma Yogi. If you do asanas for yourself, it's karma. You're not even supposed to worship for yourself. You're not supposed to meditate for yourself.

Doing for yourself is karma, not Karma Yoga; it's not a selfless action. Even if you meditate for yourself, it's a selfish act.

Everything should be based on selflessness. "Why should I meditate? What is the purpose? So I can clean the mind, calm the mind, strengthen the mind. Why? To serve well."

Then even your meditation becomes Karma Yoga. "Why should I even eat? To have enough strength and vitality to serve." Everything should ultimately be selfless service.

There is no greater Yoga than Karma Yoga. Karma Yoga is the biggest Yoga and the most difficult to practice. Remember that. You can practice all the other Yogas with ease.

But the most difficult thing is Karma Yoga, because the ego will pop up at every moment. The secret is to forget yourself, then Karma Yoga will be easy. You will be the happiest person.

Joy is Your Reward

These days we see business, business, business in everything. The whole world is embroiled in karma. Karma means labor and labor means doing something to get something in return–that's why it's laborious.

If you call something labor, it shows that you feel it's difficult or painful. I sometimes wonder why we give the name "labor" to the mother's work. We say, "She is in labor." No, there's no labor in that; it's a joy. Labor means hardship, difficulty, pain, because you want something in return.

That's the reason we come across a lot of labor mediation boards all over. When you expect something, there will always be some kind of tussle; you won't get exactly what you expected.

The boss expects more work from you and you expect more money from him. There is a continuous pull between employer and employee.

To undo these entanglements you need a labor department, labor mediators and so on. Have you ever heard of a "service mediator"? No, because there is no trouble created with service. Nobody goes to court in the name of service.

But what do we see, even in the name of marriage? The husband says, "Honey, I love you." Then he looks at her face and waits. What for? "Oh, Honey, I love you too!"

But if she doesn't say anything, what will he do? Buy a ticket to Mexico! Can we call that love then? No, it's business: "I love you so that you will love me." In true selfless love, you just love. "I love you because loving you makes me happy; that's all."

Real love and service are one-sided; you just give for the joy of giving. There's no expectation whatsoever so you never get into any troubles. Neither you have trouble nor does the one who receives your service.

When you have done someone a service, he or she will never feel an obligation if you have really done it purely as a selfless service. That is the best service possible. When you give a gift, don't make the recipient obliged to you. Don't even look at his face to see a nice smile or "thank you" or a little appreciation. No; because if you expect that smile or nod or "thank you," and you miss that, you won't be happy.

Suppose you give something and the person is so busy doing something else that she just takes it and continues what she is doing. You will be disappointed. Why? You expected something in return. Making the recipient obliged to you is itself a karma, not a Karma Yoga. Service is just doing for the sake of doing, serving for the joy of serving. That itself is the maximum and best reward you can get; nobody can stop that reward.

If you do some service to somebody and that person says, "Is that all you can do?" you can feel, "That's fine." You had the joy of giving something so you don't bother about what the person says. You wanted to give, you gave and you are happy. Can anybody stop that?

Only you can disturb that joy. How? By expecting something in return. The minute you have an expectation, you lose the joy. Your peace of mind is lost. Even before giving we build up tension: "I'm wrapping it so beautifully; she should really appreciate this." See? Even before wrapping, even before buying the gift, you are thinking of the result, so there is a tension, there are complications; you are not happy, you are not at ease doing the service.

All kinds of anxieties come in. If he says, "Honey, how beautiful; thank you very much," you are relieved. Until then you have a tension, "Will he appreciate it? Will it make him love me more?" And even later, "Did he really like it?" All these anxieties are due to your expectations.

Even if the recipient shows appreciation, your happiness will not last long if it is due to his or her appreciation that you feel happy. Then, it is just a borrowed happiness. Next, the fear of losing it comes in. You won't want anybody else to give him a present.

"Suppose someone gives a bigger, better one?" Jealousy comes in.

That's all a kind of business. Since I came to America, I have often heard the term "business gifts." You send a nice parcel today and then go with your petition tomorrow. That's not a gift, it's just business.

And we don't even spare God these "business gifts." Sometimes people light a nice beautiful candle in the church and say, "Hey, God, don't just keep on looking at that! Listen to my application. I have to run to the office soon. You can appreciate that later, but now listen to me. This is what I want from You…" We do business even in the name of God.

God's Business

Actually, God is a fair business person. As you give, you will receive. If you give 10 percent, you get only 10 percent of God's gifts. Suppose you give 100 percent, what will you get? One-hundred percent of God. Your 100 percent is worth very little. Maybe you give your 150 pounds of flesh and bone, a few ideas, feelings, your big ego, this and that.

But with all that, God doesn't care and only wants your percentage. Are you giving completely, are you surrendering totally? God only wants the surrendering. God is not going to use you; you aren't that much use to God.

God says, "What is this? This person has given 100 percent. What am I to do? I have to give my 100 percent in return." So you get 100 percent of God. Your dedication, your Karma Yoga is really a business deal–but it's a good deal!

This reminds me of a great great saint of South India named Manikkavachakar. "*Maanika*" means gem, "*vachaka*" means speech. His words were like gems.

In one of his poems he says, "God, you are not a very good business person. If You keep on doing business like this, I don't know how You will keep your business going! I seem to be much more clever than You. You gave Yourself to me in exchange for this frail little body and mind. I'm useless to You; but I'm getting everything from You. With You, I have the whole universe."

The *Bible* says, "Seek ye first the Kingdom of God." That is your first and foremost duty. Once you achieve that, what happens? The *Bible* passage continues: "Everything else will be added unto you." God gives you everything afterwards. When you are only attached to God, then God says: "OK, now you are a good child, not attached to anything else, you only love Me. I should give you everything now."

So, when God comes to you, all that belongs to God is yours. When you say there is only one God and you are the child of God, to which country do you belong?

All the countries are God's, is it not so? Not only America was created by God, Africa also. Can you say Africa is not your place then? If you deny that, you don't realize that you have a right to God's Kingdom.

As a child you are heir to it. So the entire universe is yours. "God, by getting You, I got everything; by getting me,

You got nothing. So who is clever?" And naturally, the Father or Mother will be happy and proud to hear these words from the child: "Oh, I have a wonderful child; I'm so happy."

That is the trick of Karma Yoga. When you do everything for the sake of doing, for the joy of doing, as a dedicated act for the benefit to humanity and not just for your benefit, you retain your joy.

Don't ever think you get joy by doing. No, the joy is in you always. But by keeping the heart pure through loving and giving, you retain the awareness of that joy.

Live to Serve

Everything, even your breathing should be dedicated. That doesn't mean you should stop breathing. Continue to breathe, but with the proper attitude, as a sacrifice. The very breath itself sacrifices itself to you, does it not? Let us learn from that breath.

The breath says, "I'm flowing into your lungs with all vitality and life but you send me out completely burnt; you murder me!" The air that goes in contains a lot of life.

What happens to it? You breathe it out as carbon dioxide. How is carbon produced? By burning. So your lungs are a cremation ground. Every minute you cremate your breath. And without the air's sacrifice, you can't live.

So we live by sacrifice and should live to sacrifice. If we are not going to sacrifice anything, all those elements that sacrifice themselves for our sakes are not just going to keep quiet. They will have a debit account in our names.

So we are indebted to the very nature. God or the nature has given us the life-breath, given us food, water, sun, rain and knowingly or unknowingly we are using all that constantly. In what way should we return the gift? Our lives must be joyous sacrifice.

Try to return more than you get. If somebody gives you a cup of water, wait for an opportunity to return a cup of juice to that person. If you return a cup of water, you are doing business. If you do not return anything, you are a thief. From whatever source, whether from a person or from the atmosphere, when you get something, you have to return it.

If you return just the exact amount, you are a fair business person. If you give more, you are a holy person, a Karma Yogi. You should know whether you are a thief or a business person or a yogi.

So for the sake of your own joy and peace, give more than you are given. Karma Yoga is called selfless action. But I say, a selfless action is the most selfish action.

The selfless people are the most selfish. Why? They want to be selfless because they don't want to lose their peace. What selfishness it is!

But fortunately, such selfish people bring only peace to others and no harm. Even if they don't give it, others sense it, take it and use it. When a candle burns, you may say the candle is selfish. It is not burning purposely to give you light; it is just there burning.

But by doing that, it naturally lights up everything around it. So the selfless person's "selfishness" disturbs no one and causes no loss to anyone.

There are no limits for Karma Yoga. You can do it anywhere: inside the church, outside the church, in the street, at home, wherever you are. In the train, on the plane, on the ship; there's no special time or place for that. Every time is the right time, every place the right place.

So let us live the life of Karma Yogis and thus retain the God, in the form of peace and joy, in us. When you shine with peace like that candle, not only will you expose yourself, but you will bring light to all around you.

May the God who is the Truth, who is Peace, who is Joy, who is all Virtue, who is within us and everywhere, bless us with this understanding, bless us to come together in this understanding, to live together and to make this whole world a beautiful heaven.

Let this be our constant wish and prayer.

Thank you so much.

OM Shanti Shanti Shanti.
OM Peace Peace Peace.

Sri Swami Satchidananda

Sri Swami Satchidananda was one of the first Yoga masters to bring the classical Yoga tradition to the West. He taught Yoga postures to Americans, introduced them to meditation, vegetarian diet and a more compassionate lifestyle.

During this period of cultural awakening, iconic pop artist Peter Max and a small circle of his artist friends beseeched the Swami to extend his brief stop in New York City so they could learn from him the secret of finding physical, mental and spiritual health, peace and enlightenment.

Three years later, he led some half a million American youth in chanting *OM*, when he delivered the official opening remarks at the 1969 Woodstock Music and Art Festival and he became known as "the Woodstock Guru."

The distinctive teachings he brought with him blend the physical discipline of Yoga, the spiritual philosophy of Vedantic literature and the interfaith ideals he pioneered.

These techniques and concepts influenced a generation and spawned a Yoga culture that is flourishing today. Today, over twenty million Americans practice Yoga as a means for managing stress, promoting health, slowing down the aging process and creating a more meaningful life.

The teachings of Swami Satchidananda have spread into the mainstream and thousands of people now teach Yoga. Integral Yoga is the foundation for Dr. Dean Ornish's landmark work in reversing heart disease and Dr. Michael Lerner's noted Commonweal Cancer Help program.

Today, Integral Yoga Institutes, teaching centers and certified teachers throughout the United States and abroad offer classes and training programs in all aspects of Integral Yoga.

In 1979, Sri Swamiji was inspired to establish Satchidananda Ashram–Yogaville. Based on his teachings, it is a place where people of different faiths and backgrounds can come to realize their essential oneness.

One of the focal points of Yogaville is the Light Of Truth Universal Shrine (LOTUS). This unique interfaith shrine honors the Spirit that unites all the world religions, while celebrating their diversity. People from all over the world come there to meditate and pray.

Over the years, Sri Swamiji received many honors for his public service, including the Juliet Hollister Interfaith Award presented at the United Nations and in 2002 the U Thant Peace Award.

In addition, he served on the advisory boards of many Yoga, world peace and interfaith organizations. He is the author of many books on Yoga and is the subject of the documentary, *Living Yoga: The life and teachings of Swami Satchidananda.*

In 2002, he entered *Mahasamadhi* (a God-realized soul's conscious final exit from the body).

For more information, visit: www.swamisatchidananda.org